Exercises in Gra

Grade 6

Written by T.R. Gadd, B.A., M. Ed.
Illustrated by Sean Parkes

ISBN 1-55035-593-7
Copyright 1999
Revised January 2006
All Rights Reserved * Printed in Canada

Published in the United States by:
On the Mark Press
3909 Witmer Road PMB 175
Niagara Falls, New York
14305
www.onthemarkpress.com

Published in Canada by:
S&S Learning Materials
15 Dairy Avenue
Napanee, Ontario
K7R 1M4
www.sslearning.com

Look For Other Language Units

Reading Response Forms .... Gr. 1-3

Reading Response Forms 4-6

The First 100 Sight Words:

    Multisensory Worksheets 1

Sight Word Activities 1

Creativity With Food 4-8

What's the Scoop on Words 4-6

Poetry & Creative Writing 4-6

Personal Spelling Dictionary 2-5

Building Word Families #1 (Short Vowels) 1-2

Passport to Adventure 7-8

Building Word Families #2 (Long Vowels) 2-3

How to Write an Essay 7-12

How to Write a Paragraph 5-10

How to Write a Composition 6-10

Passion of Jesus: Play 7-9

ESL Teaching Ideas K-8

Multi-Level Spelling Program 3-6

Spelling 1

Spelling 2

Spelling 3

Spelling 4

Spelling 5

Spelling 6

Exercises in Grammar 6

Exercises in Grammar 7

Exercises in Grammar 8

Spelling Blacklines 1

How to Give a Presentation 4-6

Fun With Phonics 1-3

Literature Response Forms 1-3

Literature Response Forms 4-6

Teacher's Guide to the Grade 6 Language Test 6

Teacher's Guide to the Grade 3 Test 3

Table of Contents

PART A: THE PARTS OF SPEECH

Introductory Activity 4

Nouns 5

Pronouns 17

Verbs 25

Adjectives 36

Adverbs 46

Prepositions 53

Conjunctions 60

Interjections 62

PART B: THE PARTS OF THE SENTENCE

Subject and Predicate 66

Principal and Subordinate Clauses 79

Kinds of Sentences 89

The Exercises in Grammar program has been devised to introduce a new "back-to-basics" curriculum. This resource emphasizes the teaching of the fundamentals of grammar, and the rules needed to implement it.

Recognizing that many teachers, particularly new teachers, may have gone through a school system which did not teach formal grammar, this resource attempts to simplify the grammatical process as much as possible.

This resource is the first of a series of three books called Exercises in Grammar. These books cover the grammar objectives for grades 6, 7 and 8.

Each of these books reviews the grammar taught in the earlier grades and integrates the new work into this review. The grade 6 curriculum emphasizes subordinate clauses, adjective and adverb phrases and comparison of adjectives. The lessons are set up through overheads, followed by exercises, followed by tests.

These resources should be used in conjunction with the current Language texts so that the grammar study may be integrated with the writing.

INTRODUCTORY ACTIVITY: PARTS OF SPEECH WORD SEARCH

Teachers may use this activity to reacquaint students with the names of the parts of speech.

Find the following names of the parts of speech in the word search. The names may be spelled horizontally, vertically or diagonally, frontwards or backwards.

NOUN PRONOUN	VERB PREPOSITION	ADJECTIVE CONJUNCTION	ADVERB INTERJECTION

```
I  N  T  E  R  J  E  C  T  I  O  N  C
V  O  X  D  N  X  H  O  I  H  I  I  V
T  I  Z  J  Y  Z  R  N  W  R  U  R  F
Q  T  N  A  U  C  E  J  T  I  D  H  A
C  I  N  D  A  N  E  U  B  I  C  R  M
F  S  Q  V  Y  M  D  N  P  J  N  Q  S
X  O  X  E  V  I  T  C  E  J  D  A  B
N  P  V  R  F  V  Y  T  P  S  D  L  H
A  E  F  B  N  D  N  I  A  Q  E  X  T
I  R  I  J  W  E  Q  O  M  M  Q  Y  O
L  P  R  O  N  O  U  N  Z  L  K  L  U
```

PART A: THE PARTS OF SPEECH

NOUNS

What is a noun?

A noun is a word that NAMES a person, place, thing or idea.

What are some examples of nouns?

Person	Place	Thing	Idea/Quality
Amy	Chicago	house	love
police man	city	ship	dream
girl	ocean	summer	fear
father	France	cat	happiness

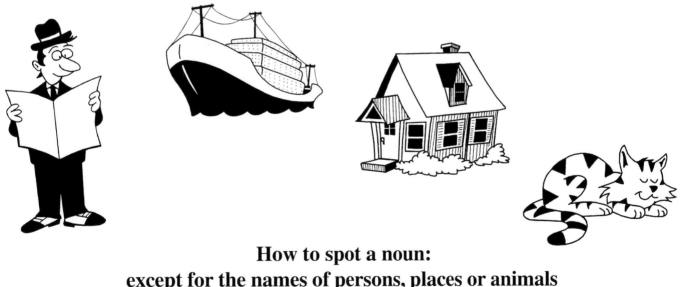

How to spot a noun:
except for the names of persons, places or animals
you can put the words "the", "a" or "an" before a noun
and it will still make sense.

PART A: THE PARTS OF SPEECH

EXERCISE 1: NOUNS

Let's see how well you can think of nouns. Fill in the chart below with as many nouns as you can think of that name each of the four categories.

Person	Place	Thing	Idea/Quality

PART A: THE PARTS OF SPEECH

NOUNS: KINDS OF NOUNS

All nouns are either COMMON or PROPER.

What is a PROPER noun?

A PROPER NOUN NAMES A <u>PARTICULAR</u> PERSON, PLACE or THING.

PROPER NOUNS ALWAYS BEGIN WITH A CAPITAL LETTER.

EXAMPLES:
Homer
Washington
Arrowhead Stadium

A COMMON NOUN DOES NOT NAME A PARTICULAR PERSON, PLACE, THING OR IDEA.

ALL NOUNS THAT ARE NOT PROPER NOUNS ARE COMMON NOUNS.

EXAMPLES:
man
country
stadium

PART A: THE PARTS OF SPEECH

EXERCISE 2: COMMON AND PROPER NOUNS

The following passage is taken from the novel, <u>The Story of Doctor Dolittle</u> by Hugh Lofting. Underline all the common nouns. Circle all the proper nouns. (Remember that proper nouns begin with capital letters, but not all words beginning with capital letters are proper nouns.)

At last, when daylight began to come through the thick leaves overhead, they heard Queen Ermintrude saying in a very tired voice that it was no use looking any more--that they might as well go back and get some sleep.

As soon as the soldiers had all gone home, Chee-Chee brought the Doctor and his animals out of the hiding place and they set off for the Land of the Monkeys.

It was a long, long way; and they often got very tired--especially Gub-Gub. But when he cried they gave him milk out of coconuts, which he was very fond of.

They always had plenty to eat and drink, because Chee-Chee and Polynesia knew all the different kinds of fruits and vegetables that grow in the jungle, and where to find them--like dates and figs and groundnuts and ginger and yams. They used to make their lemonade out of the juice of wild oranges, sweetened with honey which they got from the bees' nests in hollow trees.

PART A: THE PARTS OF SPEECH

PLURALS OF NOUNS

1. Most nouns in English form the plural by adding *s*:

Examples: dog – *dogs*, mother – *mothers*, tree – *trees*

2. Nouns ending in *s, x, ch* or *sh* form the plural by adding *es*:

Examples: mess – *messes*, box – *boxes*, branch – *branches*,
dish – *dishes*

3. Nouns ending in *y* preceded by a consonant form the plural by changing the *y* to *i* and adding *es*:

Examples: army – *armies*, sky – *skies*, butterfly – *butterflies*

4. Nouns ending in *y* preceded by a vowel form the plural by adding *s*:

Examples: boy – *boys*, day – *days*

5. Some nouns change the vowel to form a plural or even add letters:

Examples: woman – *women*, child – *children*, goose – *geese*

6. There are exceptions to most of these rules.

PART A: THE PARTS OF SPEECH

EXERCISE 3: PLURALS OF NOUNS

Make sure you have copied the rules for Plurals of Nouns from Overhead #3 into your notebook, because you will need them to complete this exercise.

In the space provided, write the plural of each of the following nouns. Next to it, write the number of the rule from Overhead #3 which accounts for the plural formation. Think of each word as: Singular: one ___; Plural: two ___--as in "one boy, two boys".

1. shark _____

2. mountain _____

3. man _____

4. child _____

5. radish _____

6. moose _____

7. president _____

8. alligator _____

9. princess _____

10. sport _____

11. toe _____

12. Christmas _____

13. river _____

14. fox _____

15. elf _____

16. farm _____

17. diary _____

18. combat _____

19. summer _____

20. lady _____

21. uncle _____

22. idea _____

23. sheep _____

24. fish _____

25. library _____

26. Spaniard _____

Overhead #4

ARNOLD THE APOSTROPHE

Poor old Arnold feels so abused and misused. Whenever they want to, writers throw him into sentences, whether he wants to go there or not!

Learn the rules for the use of the apostrophe and help Arnold to feel good about himself again.

PART A: THE PARTS OF SPEECH

POSSESSION IN NOUNS

POSSESSION MEANS:
BELONGING TO (OWNERSHIP)
OCCUPIED BY

"Gillian's desk" may mean that Gillian owns or occupies/uses the desk.

SIMPLE RULES TO FORM POSSESSION

1. TO FORM THE POSSESSIVE OF SINGULAR NOUNS, ADD 'S

EXAMPLES: The land which belongs to Graham: Graham_'s_ land
The palace in which a princess lives: princess_'s_ palace.

2. TO FORM THE POSSESSIVE OF PLURAL NOUNS WHICH END IN S, ADD '

EXAMPLES: The land which belongs to Americans: Americans_'_ land
The palace in which the Windsors live: the Windsors_'_ palace.

3. TO FORM THE POSSESSIVE OF PLURAL NOUNS WHICH DO NOT END IN S, ADD 'S

EXAMPLES: The land which belongs to women: women_'s_ land
The palace in which the people live: the people_'s_ palace.

PART A: THE PARTS OF SPEECH

EXERCISE 4: POSSESSIVE NOUNS

Rewrite each of the following phrases using an apostrophe and a possessive noun.

Example: dresses for girls: girls' dresses.

1. the rules of the game
2. the footprints of the deer
3. letters written by Nelson Mandela
4. the record by the Spice Girls
5. the testimony of the witness
6. the sister of Laura
7. the lamp which Aladdin found
8. a playground for children
9. the biggest mistake made by Olive
10. the moon of Jupiter
11. the city where Lincoln lived
12. lies my brother told
13. the house where John lives
14. the litter box for my cat
15. the speed of the ball
16. the message of the story
17. the roof of the building
18. the passengers on *Titanic*
19. a dream that Ryan has
20. the mother of Charles

1. _____
2. _____
3. _____
4. _____
5. _____
6. _____
7. _____
8. _____
9. _____
10. _____
11. _____
12. _____
13. _____
14. _____
15. _____
16. _____
17. _____
18. _____
19. _____
20. _____

EXERCISE 5: POSSESSIVE NOUNS

Circle the possessive noun in each sentence which follows.

1. The Spice Girls' new CD is now the biggest selling CD in North America.

2. England won the World Cup game because of Michael Owens' strategic plays.

3. Diana has often been called "the people's princess".

4. Carlene's grandmother made her a new dress.

5. Marissa decided to decorate the boxes' lids.

6. President Roosevelt denounced the enemy's attack on Pearl Harbor.

7. The scientist clipped the goose's wings to prevent it from flying.

8. All of the knives' edges appeared to be blunt.

EXERCISE 6: POSSESSIVE NOUNS

The following passage contains six words using the apostrophe. Four of these are used correctly; two are not. Write each word in the blank provided. Tell if the apostrophe is used correctly or incorrectly. If it is used incorrectly, write the word correctly.

The animals lived quietly in the jungle before human beings arrived. Of course, the tigers' dinner was often a stray gazelle, but the birds' nests were high in the trees where the snake's couldn't get them, and the giraffes' vegetarian diet left even the smallest canary's to live in safe surroundings. The elephants and the monkeys lived in peace together, even in the shadow of the lions' den.

1. _____   4. _____

2. _____   5. _____

3. _____   6. _____

EXERCISE 7: FUN WITH NOUNS

In the chart below, change **LAMB** to **PINE** in four steps. To complete this puzzle you must follow two rules: change only one letter in each row and use only nouns--no other part of speech is allowed. Watch out for verbs--coming soon!

L	A	M	B
P	I	N	E

EXERCISE 8: FUN WITH NOUNS

Write a noun in the first row across. Then, as if you are creating a crossword, write nouns that intersect with this row. Keep adding nouns, but make sure that when you have two or more letters in a row that they make a complete word. Try to fill in as much of the crossword as you can.

PART A: THE PARTS OF SPEECH
ANSWERS TO EXERCISES ON NOUNS

Exercise 2: *(page 8)*

At last, when **daylight** began to come through the thick **leaves** overhead, they head (Queen Ermintrude) saying in a very tired **voice** that it was no use looking any more--that they might as well go back and get some **sleep**.

As soon as the **soldiers** had all gone **home**, (Chee-Chee) brought the (Doctor) and his **animals** out of the hiding **place** and they se toff for the (Land of the Monkeys)

It was a long, long **way**; and they often got very tired--especially (Gub-Gub) But when he cried they gave him **milk** out of **coconuts**, which he was very fond of.

They always had plenty to eat and drink, because (Chee-Chee) and (Polynesia) knew all the different **kinds** of **fruits** and **vegetables** that grow in the **jungle**, and where to find them--like **dates** and **figs** and **groundnuts** and **ginger** and **yams**. They used to make their **lemonade** out of the **juice** of wild **oranges**, sweetened with **honey** which they got from the **bees' nests** in hollow **trees**.

Exercise 3: *(page 10)*

1. sharks	2. mountains	3. men	4. children	5. radishes
6. moose	7. presidents	8. alligators	9. princesses	10. sports
11. toes	12. Christmases	13. rivers	14. foxes	15. elves
16. farms	17. diaries	18. combats	19. summers	20. ladies
21. uncles	22. ideas	23. sheep	24. fish (or fishes)	25. ibraries
26. Spaniards				

Exercise 4: *(page 13)*

1. the game's rules	2. the deer's footprints	3. Nelson Mandela's letters
4. the Spice Girls' record	5. the witness's testimony	6. Laura's sister
7. Aladdin's lamp	8. a children's playground	9. Olive's biggest mistake
10. Jupiter's moon	11. Lincoln's city	12. my brother's lies
13. John's house	14. my cat's little box	15. the ball's speed
16. the story's message	17. the building's room	18. *Titanic's* passengers
19. Ryan's dream	20. Charles's mother.	

Exercise 5: *(page 14)*

1. Spice Girls'	2. Michael Owens'	3. people's	4. Carlene's	5. boxes'	6. enemy's
7. goose's	8. knives'				

Exercise 6: *(page 14)*

1. tigers' – correct	2. birds' – correct	3. snake's – incorrect: snakes
4. giraffes' – correct	5. canary's – incorrect: canaries	6. lions' – correct.

Exercise 7: *(page 15)*

L	A	M	B
L	I	M	B
L	I	M	E
L	I	N	E
P	I	N	E

Overhead #6

PRONOUNS

What is a pronoun?

A pronoun is a word that **REPLACES** a noun.

If we had no pronouns, we would have to use nouns again and again in sentences. This would become very repetitive and very annoying to read.

What are some examples of pronouns?

I, you, he, she, it, we, you, they
everyone, someone, nobody
their, itself

The noun which the pronoun replaces is called its

ANTECEDENT

What are some examples of pronouns and their antecedents?

ANTECEDENT	PRONOUN
Marsha	she, her, herself
airline pilot	he, his, himself
cat	it, he, she, its, himself

PART A: THE PARTS OF SPEECH

Overhead #7

KINDS OF PRONOUNS

There are several kinds of pronouns but the most common is the

PERSONAL PRONOUN

A personal pronoun is a word that **REPLACES a noun** by referring to what grammarians call

PERSON

There are three **PERSONS** in grammar:

1. first person: the person speaking (I, we)

2. second person: the person spoken to (you)

3. third person: the person or thing spoken about (he, she, it, they)

Notice that each person has several forms and we use these forms differently in our sentences:

> I, my, me, we, our, ours, us
> you, your, yours
> he, his, him
> she, her, hers
> it, its
> they, their, theirs, them.

EXERCISE 8: PERSONAL PRONOUNS

Circle the personal pronouns in each of the following sentences. Then draw an arrow to the antecedent of the pronoun:

1. Jessica asked her father to buy her a horse.

2. *Titanic* sank on its maiden voyage and many of its passengers died.

3. Chris, please do your work to the best of your ability.

4. Potatoes are called *pommes de terre* in France because they resemble apples.

5. When Columbus reached the New World, he thought he had sailed to India.

EXERCISE 9: PERSONAL PRONOUNS

Fill in the bubble with what you think the character might say. Use at least one personal pronoun in your dialog. Underline all personal pronouns.

PART A: THE PARTS OF SPEECH

Overhead #8

KINDS OF PRONOUNS

Other kinds of pronouns:

POSSESSIVE PRONOUNS

A possessive pronoun is a form of personal pronoun which shows ownership.

EXAMPLES
my, mine, our, ours, your, yours,
his, her, hers, its,
their, theirs

Note that possessive pronouns do not use the apostrophe to form possession.

REFLEXIVE PRONOUNS

A reflexive pronoun is another form of the personal pronoun which reflects back on or refers to itself.

EXAMPLES
myself, ourselves,
yourselves, himself,
herself, itself, themselves

PART A: THE PARTS OF SPEECH

Overhead #9

KINDS OF PRONOUNS
Continued

DEMONSTRATIVE PRONOUNS

A demonstrative pronoun is used to point out a specific, person or thing.

EXAMPLES
this, that, these, those.

INDEFINITE PRONOUNS

An indefinite pronoun does not refer to a definite person or thing and may be used without an antecedent.

EXAMPLES
each, either, someone, no one, everyone, something, anything

INTERROGATIVE PRONOUNS

An interrogative pronoun asks a question.

EXAMPLES
**Who…? Whom…? Whose…?
What…? Which…?**

PART A: THE PARTS OF SPEECH

EXERCISE 10: KINDS OF PRONOUNS

Each of the following sentences contains one pronoun. In the chart which follows, write the pronoun, tell its antecedent, and state what kind of pronoun it is.

1. Mourab came to Boston from Ghana, where he was born.
2. Who was the first person to climb Mount Everest?
3. Mom will cook the dinner herself before the game starts.
4. Anyone with knowledge of the incident should see the principal.
5. Mrs. Ferguson wanted her instructions to be carried out carefully.
6. "Don't do that!" said Oliver to Elizabeth.
7. Terry Fox will be remembered for his courage for many years to come.
8. The scuba divers might have scratched themselves on the coral in the reef.
9. The teacher said to the class, "This is the next project for homework."
10. Somebody ought to change the way people think about other people.

Number	Pronoun	Antecedent	Kind of Pronoun
1.			
2.			
3.			
4.			
5.			
6.			
7.			
8.			
9.			
10.			

PART A: THE PARTS OF SPEECH

REVIEW TEST #1: NOUNS AND PRONOUNS (20 marks)

A) Read the following passage. In the space provided, tell whether the underlined word is: (**10 marks**)

- a common noun
- a personal pronoun
- a reflexive pronoun
- an indefinite pronoun

- a proper noun
- a possessive pronoun
- a demonstrative pronoun
- an interrogative pronoun

"**What** shall we do?" asked **Dorothy**, despairingly.

"**I** haven't the slightest idea," said the **Tin Woodman**; and the Lion shook his shaggy **mane** and looked thoughtful. But the Scarecrow said: "We cannot fly, that is certain; neither can we climb down into this great ditch **ourselves**. Therefore, if we cannot jump over it, we must stop where we are."

"I think I could jump over **it**," said the Cowardly Lion, after measuring the **distance** carefully in his mind.

"Then we are all right," answered the Scarecrow, "for you can carry us all over on **your** back, **one** at a time."

1. what _____
2. Dorothy _____
3. I _____
4. Tin Woodman _____
5. mane _____

6. ourselves _____
7. it _____
8. distance _____
9. your _____
10. one _____

B) Write the plural of each of the following nouns in the space provided. (**5 marks**)

1. rive _____
2. princess _____
3. child _____

4. moose _____
5. library _____

C) Write the possessive of each of the following nouns in the space provided. (**5 marks**)

1. Aladdin _____
2. princesses _____
3. sister _____

4. stories _____
5. deer _____

PART A: THE PARTS OF SPEECH
ANSWERS TO EXERCISES ON PRONOUNS

Exercise 8: (page 19)
1. Jessica asked **her** father to buy **her** a horse. *Antecedent:* ***Jessica***
2. *Titanic* sank on **its** maiden voyage and many of <u>its</u> passengers died. *Antecedent:* ***Titanic***
3. Chris, please do **your** work to the best of **your** ability. *Antecedent:* ***Chris***
4. Potatoes are called *pommes de terre* in France because **they** resemble apples.
   Antecedent: ***Potatoes***
5. When Columbus reached the New World, **he** thought **he** had sailed to India.
   Antecedent: ***Columbus***

Exercise 10: (page 22)

Number	Pronoun	Antecedent	Kind of Pronoun
1	he	Mourab	Personal
2	Who	no antecedent	Interrogative
3	herself	Mom	Reflexive
4	Anyone	no antecedent	Indefinite
5	her	Mrs. Ferguson	Possessive
6	that	no antecedent	Demonstrative
7	his	Terry Fox	Possessive
8	themselves	scuba divers	Reflexive
9	This	project	Demonstrative
10	Somebody	no antecedent	Indefinite

Preview Test #1: (page 23)

A)
1. what — <u>demonstrative pronoun</u>
2. Dorothy — <u>proper noun</u>
3. I — <u>personal pronoun</u>
4. Tin Woodman — <u>proper noun</u>
5. mane — <u>common noun</u>
6. ourselves — <u>reflexive pronoun</u>
7. it — <u>personal pronoun</u>
8. distance — <u>common noun</u>
9. your — <u>possessive pronoun</u>
10. one — <u>indefinite pronoun</u>

B)
1. river — <u>rivers</u>
2. princess — <u>princesses</u>
3. child — <u>children</u>
4. moose — <u>moose</u>
5. library — <u>libraries</u>

C)
1. Aladdin — <u>Aladdin's</u>
2. princesses — <u>princesses'</u>
3. sister — <u>sister's</u>
4. stories — <u>stories'</u>
5. deer — <u>deer's</u>

PART A: THE PARTS OF SPEECH

Overhead #10

> ## VERBS

What is a VERB?

Generally, a verb is a word that shows ACTION.

What are some examples of verbs that show action?

> ## ACTION VERBS
>
> | | |
> |---|---|
> | run | sing |
> | speak | laugh |
> | swim | choose |
> | flight | fly |

Some verbs do not show action.
Instead, they show a state of being.
These verbs are called NON-ACTION, or BEING or LINKING VERBS.

What are some examples of linking verbs?

> ## NON-ACTION VERBS
>
> is, are, was, were
> seem
> taste
> appear
> become

PART A: THE PARTS OF SPEECH

Overhead #11

VERB PHRASES

What is a VERB PHRASE?

A PHRASE is a group of related words.
A VERB PHRASE is a MAIN VERB with one or more HELPING VERBS.

EXAMPLES OF HELPING VERBS:
1. all forms of the verb BE: be, am, are, is, was, were
2. forms of the verb HAVE: has, have, had
3. forms of the verb BE ABLE: can, could
4. forms of the verb DO: do, does, did
5. shall, will, should, would
6. might, must

EXAMPLES OF VERB PHRASES IN SENTENCES:
1. Anthony <u>is returning</u> to Jamaica this summer.
2. A polar bear <u>may weigh</u> 500 pounds.
3. Adventure movies <u>have</u> always <u>appealed</u> to Jane.
4. I <u>have eaten</u> all my spinach.

PART A: THE PARTS OF SPEECH

EXERCISE 11: RECOGNIZING VERBS

Underline the verbs in each of the following sentences.

1. Diseases such as yellow fever killed more people than bullets did in the Spanish-American War.

2. In 1898, Dr. William Gorgas, who lived in Havana, Cuba, killed many of the mosquitoes that carried the yellow fever virus.

3. Gorgas accomplished this task because he arranged for the cleaning of the streets in Havana.

4. In Panama City, Gorgas fumigated every building and rid the city of the virus in less than two years.

5. People built the Panama Canal because they stayed healthy.

6. King George V knighted Gorgas for his work.

EXERCISE 12: VERBS AND VERB PHRASES

Underline the verbs and verb phrases in each of the following sentences.

1. Malaria was a bigger challenge to Dr. Gorgas because it was carried by mosquitoes which lived in the jungle.

2. Through a narrow strip of land where the Panama Canal was planned, Gorgas organized crews of people who eliminated swamps and burned insecticide.

3. Because of his efforts, the narrow strip of land was cleared of the malaria mosquitoes and the crews could build the canal.

4. President Theodore Roosevelt gave Gorgas a promotion for his great success.

EXERCISE 13: ACTION AND LINKING VERBS

Underline the verb or verb phrase in each of the following sentences. In the blank provided, identify each as an action verb or a linking verb.

1. Hansel and Gretel sat by the fire. _____

2. At dinnertime, they each ate their little slice of bread. _____

3. They thought their father was quite near. _____ _____

4. They could hear the sound of an ax. _____

5. It was not an ax, however, but the sound of a tree branch. _____

6. Soon they became tired and fell asleep. _____ _____

7. When they awoke, it was night. _____ _____

8. When the full moon rose, Hansel took his little sister's hand, and they walked through the woods. _____ _____ _____

9. They walked the whole night long, and at daybreak they were back at their father's cottage. _____ _____

10. They knocked at the door of the cottage and their mean, old stepmother opened it for them. _____ _____

PART A: THE PARTS OF SPEECH

EXERCISE 14: USING VERBS

Finish each sentence which follows by writing a verb in the blank space provided. Try to use a verb which expresses a precise meaning. Try to avoid using dull or ordinary verbs like "is", "are", "was", "were".

1. At the World Championships, the Judges _____ the highest marks to the Russian skater.

2. When I tried to enter, Juanita _____ the door.

3. It _____ all afternoon.

4. Some of the children who came to the door on Halloween _____ horrible masks.

5. Without warning, the Alien from Another Planet _____.

6. Jackie _____ everything.

7. Twenty-two students in my class _____ the roller coaster at the amusement park.

8. A.Y. Jackson _____ Algonquin Park many times during his long career as an artist.

9. Many people still _____ *Gone With The Wind* more than 60 years after the movie was released.

10. Carmelita _____ to her friends.

11. Three goats _____ in the fields all afternoon.

12. Wyatt Earp _____ the outlaws at the O.K. Corral.

13. Henry Ford _____ the automobile, so now many people are able to drive it.

14. Mrs. Lynch _____ the students who did well on the test.

Overhead #12

VERB TENSES

What is a VERB TENSE?

A verb expresses an action.

A tense tells the <u>TIME</u> when the action takes place.

Many verb tenses are formed from the INFINITIVE.

What is an INFINITIVE?

An INFINITIVE is
a VERB FORM
beginning with "TO".
examples:
to live   to ride   to laugh

In your notebook, make a list of ten infinitives.

Here are some examples:

to say

to eat

to play

to think

PART A: THE PARTS OF SPEECH

VERB TENSES

THE SIMPLE TENSES

The SIMPLE TENSES are the simplest form of the verb:

There are three Simple Tenses. They are:

PRESENT   PAST   FUTURE.

The SIMPLE PRESENT TENSE *is* formed from the infinitive.

Present Tense: I live, I ride, I laugh.

The SIMPLE PAST TENSE *is not* formed from the infinitive.

Past Tense: I lived, I rode, I laughed.

The SIMPLE FUTURE TENSE *is* formed from the infinitive.

Future Tense: I shall live, I shall ride, I shall laugh

--or--I will live, I will ride, I will laugh.

Overhead #14

CONSISTENT VERB TENSES

Tenses show the time RELATIONSHIP between actions which occur in sentences.

Writers use the <u>SAME</u> verb tense when actions occur at the same time.

If a writer uses both the past tense and the present tense in the same sentence, the writer indicates that the action in the past occurred <u>*before*</u> the action in the present.

Example: *I speak to John and told him* would be incorrect because these actions occurred at the same time.
The correct sentence would read:
I spoke to John and told him.

I went up to him and I says…
is similarly incorrect
because both actions occurred in the past.

I read the book and now I know more about the subject
would be correct
because the reading occurred in the past
and the knowing in the present.

EXERCISE 15: VERB TENSES

In the blank provided write the simple present tense of the verb *to be*.

1. Whenever I _____ tired, I go to sleep
2. Fifty seven people _____ ahead of me in the line.
3. My mother _____ the best friend I have.
4. You _____ very good at Mathematics.
5. We _____ going to the zoo on Saturday.

EXERCISE 16: VERB TENSES

In the blank provided, write the form of the verb required.

1. **ask** (*simple past*)
   Marc _____ if I had ever visited Disney Land.
2. **give** (*simple past*)
   My grandfather _____ me a souvenir of the war.
3. **come** (*simple present*)
   I will speak to her when she _____ home.
4. **see** (*simple present*)
   A cat _____ in the dark.
5. **eat** (*simple past*)
   Waldo _____ his lunch in the school cafeteria.
6. **begin** (*simple past*)
   The doctor _____ by examining my chest.
7. **dust** (*simple past*)
   The custodian _____ the shelves each week.
8. **use** (*simple present*)
   Peter _____ hinges to mount his stamps.
9. **attack** (*simple past*)
   William of Normandy _____ England in 1066.
10. **risk** (*simple past*)
    A fireman _____ his life every day.
11. **drown** (*simple past*)
    Very few people _____ when *Titanic* sank.
12. **know** (*simple past*)

    I _____ the answers to all the questions on the test.

PART A: THE PARTS OF SPEECH

REVIEW TEST #2: VERBS (20 marks)

1. There are five verbs or verb phrases in the following paragraph. Underline each one. Be sure to underline the entire verb phrase, but no additional words. (**5 marks**)

Most of my family live in Wales, where I was born. All of the country is very beautiful with mountains and hills and valleys everywhere. Some of my relatives work in industrial jobs, while others perform professional duties.

2. In the space provided, identify the underlined verb or verb phrase as action verb or linking verb. (**5 marks**)

   a) The moon **rose** early on that fateful night! _____

   b) Brenda **is** an excellent soccer player. _____

   c) My neighbor's dog **barks** at everyone who passes by. _____

   d) The prisoners **climbed** over the wall to escape. _____

   e) Marvin **was** the first badge winner in Scouts. _____

3. In the blank provided, write the present tense of the verb *to be*. (**5 marks**)

   a) When I _____ good, everyone is happy.

   b) People _____ sometimes cruel to animals.

   c) Paula _____ a very good friend of my sister.

   d) You _____ the winner in this lottery.

   e) We _____ always well behaved.

4. In the blank provided, write the form of the verb required. (**5 marks**)

   a) come (*simple present*)   Friends _____ to visit me often.

   b) use (*simple present*)   The artist _____ color very well.

   c) begin (*simple past*)   The team _____ to play without me.

   d) eat (*simple past*)   The whole family _____ dinner on the plane.

   e) have (*simple past*)   We _____ all our provisions in the hamper.

PART A: THE PARTS OF SPEECH

ANSWERS TO EXERCISES ON VERBS

Exercise 11: *(page 27)*
1. Diseases such as yellow fever **killed** more people than bullets **did** in the Spanish-American War.
2. In 1898, Dr. William Gorgas, who **lived** in Havana, Cuba, **killed** many of the mosquitoes that **carried** the yellow fever virus.
3. Gorgas **accomplished** this task because he **arranged** for the cleaning of the streets in Havana.
4. In Panama City, Gorgas **fumigated** every building and **rid** the city of the virus in less than two years.
5. People **built** the Panama Canal because they **stayed** healthy.
6. King George V **knighted** Gorgas for his work.

Exercise 12: *(page 27)*
1. Malaria **was** a bigger challenge to Dr. Gorgas because it **was carried** by mosquitoes which **lived** in the jungle.
2. Through a narrow strip of land where the Panama Canal **was planned**, Gorgas **organized** crews of people who **eliminated** swamps and **burned** insecticide.
3. Because of his efforts, the narrow strip of land **was cleared** of the malaria mosquitoes and the crews **could build** the canal.
4. President Theodore Roosevelt **gave** Gorgas a promotion for his great success.

Exercise 13: *(page 28)*
1. sat: action
2. ate: action
3. thought: action   was: linking
4. could hear: action
5. was: copula
6. became: copula   fell: action
7. awoke: action   was: copula
8. rose: action   took: action walked: action
9. walked: action   were: copula
10. knocked: action   opened: action.

Exercise 14: *(page 29)*
Answers will vary.

Exercise 15: *(page 33)*
1. am   2. are   3. is   4. are   5. are

Exercise 16: *(page 33)*
1. asked   2. gave   3. comes   4. sees   5. ate   6. began   7. dusted
8. uses   9. attacked   10. risks   11. drowned   12. knew

Review Test #2: *(page 34)*
1. live, was born, is, work, perform
2. **a)** action   **b)** linking   **c)** action   **d)** action   **e)** linking
3. **a)** am   **b)** are   **c)** is   **d)** are   **e)** are
4. **a)** come   **b)** uses   **c)** began   **d)** ate   **e)** had

Overhead #15

ADJECTIVES

What is an ADJECTIVE?

An adjective is a word which describes or modifies a noun.

What does *modify* mean?

Essentially, *to modify* means *to change*.

When we say that an adjective modifies a noun
we mean that the adjective changes the noun in some way.

Example:
Noun: a man
Notice how each adjective modifies or changes
the image of the noun:
an *old* man
a *young* man
a *handsome* man
an *ugly* man
a *fat* man
a *thin* man
a *stingy* man
a *generous* man.

In each case the reader's image of the man has been changed or
modified by
the writer's choice of adjective.

PART A: THE PARTS OF SPEECH

EXERCISE 17: RECOGNIZING ADJECTIVES

Underline the adjectives in each of the following sentences. Then draw an arrow from each adjective to the noun it modifies.

1. An angry child is not a happy child.

2. It was a dark and stormy night.

3. My grandmother cannot stand loud music because it hurts her sensitive ears.

4. Because Charles Dickens came from a poor family, he never received a formal education.

5. Good dishwashers will even clean the greasiest plates.

6. Elaine's favorite sport is hockey because she likes the fast pace of the game.

7. When we first saw Rags, he was the dirtiest dog we had ever seen.

8. Giant tortoises can live for many years.

9. Aladdin was a young beggar whose future was changed when he found an old lamp in a strange, dark cave.

10. *The Simpsons* is one of the funniest shows on television.

11. The moon is a ghostly galleon tossed upon cloudy seas.

12. Winnie-the-Pooh is a cute little bear which small children love.

13. Dumbo was a stubborn elephant who became the lovable star of the circus.

14. Last summer, we enjoyed staying in our rustic cottage where we watched the gold and red sun set over the lake.

15. Mr. Jones grows luscious tomatoes and beans in his garden.

PART A: THE PARTS OF SPEECH

EXERCISE 18: USING ADJECTIVES

In the space provided, write three adjectives which could modify each of the following nouns.

1. a student:

_____   _____   _____

2. a horse:

_____   _____   _____

3. a movie you like:

_____   _____   _____

4. a T.V. show you don't like:

_____   _____   _____

5. an athlete:

_____   _____   _____

EXERCISE 19: USING ADJECTIVES

Make a list of **ten** adjectives which you think describe you very well. Then write a five line poem about yourself. Use your own name as the first and fifth lines, two adjectives in the second and fourth lines, and three adjectives in the third line.

Here is an example:

Barbara
Elegant, graceful,
Stubborn, pushy, forceful,
Intelligent, determined,
Barbara.

EXERCISE 20: USING ADJECTIVES

In groups of three or four, make a list of ten adjectives which could describe the man in the picture. Choose your best adjective to present to the class. Then have the class decide which adjective from all the groups is the most appropriate choice.

List the adjectives here:

1. _____

2. _____

3. _____

4. _____

5. _____

6. _____

7. _____

8. _____

9. _____

10. _____

Rewrite your group's choice of best adjective here:

_____

Overhead #16

COMPARISON OF ADJECTIVES

What does COMPARISON mean?

If we *compare* two things, we show how they are alike.
Adjectives may help us to *compare* two or more nouns.
Example: Mary is <u>taller</u> than her brother.

DEGREES OF COMPARISON

There are three degrees of comparison:

1. POSITIVE: shows no comparison:
Example: Mary is <u>tall</u>.

2. COMPARATIVE: compares two nouns:
Example: Mary is <u>taller</u> than her brother.

3. SUPERLATIVE: compares three or more nouns:
Example: Mary is the <u>tallest</u> in her family.

FORMING COMPARISONS: REGULAR ADJECTIVES

Normally we form the Comparative Degree by adding *er* to an adjective.

Normally we form the Superlative Degree by adding *est* to an adjective.

EXERCISE 21: COMPARISON OF REGULAR ADJECTIVES

Complete the chart with the positive, comparative or superlative degree of the adjective.

Positive	Comparative	Superlative
1. big		
2.	sharper	
3.		oldest
4. hot		
5.	longer	
6. poor		
7.		prettiest
8. short		
9.		highest
10. funny		

EXERCISE 22: COMPARISON OF REGULAR ADJECTIVES

In the space provided, write three sentences, using the positive, comparative and superlative degrees (one in each sentence) of either: **heavy** or **fast**.

1. _____

   _____

2. _____

   _____

3. _____

   _____

Overhead #17

COMPARISON OF IRREGULAR ADJECTIVES

Although most adjectives form
the Comparative Degree by adding *er*
and the Superlative Degree by adding *est*,
some do not:
These are IRREGULAR adjectives.

IRREGULAR ADJECTIVES
form the Comparative by adding the word **MORE**
and the Superlative by adding the word **MOST**.

Example: *courteous, more courteous, most courteous*

It would be silly to say *courteouser* or *courteousest*.
Some regular adjectives may also form comparison in this way:
friendly, friendlier, friendliest is correct
so is: *friendly, more friendly, most friendly*.

Some **IRREGULAR ADJECTIVES** change form completely.

Examples: *good, better, best* or *bad, worse, worst*.

Some **ADJECTIVES** cannot be compared.

Example: *Unique* means *one of a kind*. Therefore, nothing
can be *more unique* or *unique*.

EXERCISE 23: USING ADJECTIVES CORRECTLY

In the blank provided, write the correct form of the adjective stated before each sentence.

1. *bad*   I played monopoly even _____ the second time.

2. *happy*   Anthony looks _____ than Joe in this picture.

3. *successful*   *Titanic* was the _____ movie in Hollywood history.

4. *heavy*   Is a kilogram of lead _____ than a kilogram of feathers?

5. *rich*   My culture has one of the _____ traditions in the world.

6. *good*   Erin's mark in Science is usually her _____.

7. *small*   The amoeba is probably the _____ living creature.

8. *cheap*   Volkswagen used to make the _____ cars in Canada.

9. *expensive*   The Hope Diamond is perhaps the _____ jewel.

10. *effective*   My doctor wanted me to try a _____ treatment.

11. *famous*   Agatha Christie is probably the _____ mystery writer in the world.

12. *young*   Geraldine is the _____ of the two sisters.

13. *simple*   Alicia looks for the _____ solution to the problem.

14. *wise*   As Marvin grew older, he became _____.

15. *neat*   Maria's work is _____ than mine.

16. *useful*   A vacuum cleaner is _____ than a broom.

17. *tall*   The CN Tower is the _____ structure in the world.

18. *kind*   My grandfather is the _____ man I have ever known.

19. *intelligent* A pig is _____ than a goat.

20. *tough*   This is the _____ problem I have ever faced.

REVIEW TEST #3: ADJECTIVES *(20 marks)*

1. Underline the adjective in each of the following sentences. Then draw an arrow to the noun it modifies: (**8 marks**)

   a) William Shakespeare was a famous poet even before he wrote plays.

   b) Avalanches can cause great problems for skiers.

   c) I have always disliked being in a dark room.

   d) Don't cry over spilled milk.

2. Fill in the chart with the comparative and superlative degrees of the adjectives listed. (**6 marks**)

Positive	Comparative	Superlative
a) small		
b) good		
c) happy		

3. In the blank provided, write the correct form of the adjective stated before each sentence. (**6 marks**)

   a) *cheap*   A VCR is _____ than a television set.

   b) *bad*   Tuesday was the _____ day of my life.

   c) *useful*   The _____ tool in my kit is the hammer.

   d) *young*   Arlene is the _____ student in the class.

   e) *sharp*   The bread knife is the _____ one we own.

   f) *expensive*   Diamonds are _____ than gold.

PART A: THE PARTS OF SPEECH

ANSWERS TO EXERCISES ON ADJECTIVES

Exercise 17: *(page 37)*
1. An **angry** child is not a **happy** child. (*child, child*)
2. It was a **dark** and **stormy** night. (*night*)
3. My grandmother cannot stand **loud** music because it hurts her **sensitive** ears. (*music, ears*)
4. Because Charles Dickens came from a **poor** family, he never received a **formal** education. (*family, education*)
5. **Good** dishwashers will even clean the **greasiest** plates. (*dishwashers, plates*)
6. Elaine's **favorite** sport is hockey because she likes the **fast** pace of the game. (*sport, pace*)
7. When we first saw Rags, he was the **dirtiest** dog we had ever seen. (*dog*)
8. **Giant** tortoises can live for **many** years. (*tortoises, years*: **Note** *"giant" may be considered part of the proper noun*)
9. Aladdin was a **young** beggar whose future was changed when he found an **old** lamp in a **strange**, **dark** cave. (*beggar, lamp, cave*)
10. *The Simpsons* is one of the **funniest** shows on television. (*shows*)
11. The moon is a **ghostly** galleon tossed upon **cloudy** seas. (*galleon, seas*)
12. Winnie-the-Pooh is a **cute little** bear which **small** children love. (*bear, children*)
13. Dumbo was a **stubborn** elephant who became the **lovable** star of the circus. (*elephant, star*)
14. **Last** summer, we enjoyed staying in our **rustic** cottage where we watched the **gold** and **red** sun set over the lake. (*summer, cottage, sun*)
15. Mr. Jones grows **luscious** tomatoes and beans in his garden. (*tomatoes*)

Exercise 21: *(page 41)*

Positive	Comparative	Superlative
1. **big**	*bigger*	*biggest*
2. *sharp*	**sharper**	*sharpest*
3. *old*	*older*	**oldest**
4. **hot**	*hotter*	*hottest*
5. *long*	**longer**	*longest*
6. **poor**	*poorer*	*poorest*
7. *pretty*	*prettier*	**prettiest**
8. **short**	*shorter*	*shortest*
9. *high*	*higher*	**highest**
10. **funny**	*funnier*	*funniest*

Exercise 23: *(page 43)*

1. worse	2. happier	3. most successful	4. heavier	5. richest
6. best	7. smallest	8. cheapest	9. most expensive	10. more effective
11. most famous	12. younger	13. simplest	14. wiser	15. neater
16. more useful	17. tallest	18. kindest	19. more intelligent	20. toughest

Review Test #3: *(page 44)*
(1 mark for adjective, 1 mark for noun)
1. a) **famous** poet   b) **great** problems   c) **dark** room   d) **spilled** milk.
2. a) smaller, smallest   b) better, best   c) happier, happiest
3. a) cheaper   b) worst   c) most useful   d) youngest
   e) sharpest   f) more expensive

Overhead #18

ADVERBS

What is an ADVERB?

An adverb is a word which describes or modifies a verb.
It may also modify an adjective or another adverb.

Remember that *to modify* means *to change*.

When we say that an adverb modifies a verb
we mean that the adverb changes the verb in some way.

Example: Verb: to run
Notice how each adverb modifies or changes the verb:
to run *quickly*
to run *slowly*
to run *effortlessly*
to run *recklessly*.

In each case the reader's image of the running has been changed or
modified by the writer's choice of adverb.

Note that the adverbs used in the examples above all end in *ly*.
We form many adverbs by adding *ly* to an adjective.
However, please note that some adjectives also end in *ly*.
Examples: *lovely, friendly, lonely*.
Similarly, some adverbs do not end in *ly*.
Examples: *now, then, often, soon, later*.

Overhead #19

HOW ADVERBS WORK

**It is easy to spot an ADVERB because adverbs answer
one of several questions to a verb.
These questions are:** *when? where? how? how much?*

Examples:

WHEN? did my work *yesterday*. (answers when? to *did*) Agatha spoke *immediately*. (answers when? to *spoke*) Henry moved *immediately*. (answers when? to *moved*)	**HOW?** I did my work *badly*. (answers how? to *did*) Agatha spoke *rudely*. (answers how? to *spoke*) Henry *happily* moved. (answers how? to *moved*)
WHERE? I did my work *here*. (answers where? to *did*) Agatha spoke *in the hall*. (answers where? to *spoke*) Henry moved *back*. (answers where? to *moved*)	**HOW MUCH?** I *barely* did my work. (answers how much? to *did*) Agatha spoke *too* much. (answers how much? to *spoke*) Henry *scarcely* moved. (answers how much? to *moved*)

PART A: THE PARTS OF SPEECH

EXERCISE 24: IDENTIFYING ADVERBS

Circle the adverbs in each of the following sentences. Draw an arrow to the verb the adverb modifies.

1. The little children waited patiently for Santa Claus to arrive on Christmas Eve.

2. "I know the answer," the game show contestant shouted excitedly.

3. Eventually the rocket rose steadily into the sky.

4. The ship sank instantly after hitting the iceberg.

5. Yesterday, Trudy worked steadily on her English exercises.

6. Because Jason plays basketball well, he has been selected for the school team.

7. At the recital, Vera danced gracefully and the audience applauded loudly.

8. My class went to the museum today.

9. Thomas read the novel carefully, so he was able to answer the questions accurately.

10. The accident occurred when the car in front of us stopped unexpectedly.

11. The problems of the environment deeply concern all human beings.

12. Joe sat quietly eating his sandwich.

13. After he went there, David developed an interest in California.

14. Mother promised she would mail my letter tomorrow if she had the time.

15. Ron arrived promptly for his interview with Mr. Jones.

16. Professional athletes train vigorously for the upcoming season.

17. George honestly believed he would see us later.

18. Susan sat nervously waiting for the examination to begin.

19. Sheila walked elegantly into the room and took her chair.

20. Bert told the joke slowly until he reached the punch-line at the end.

EXERCISE 25: USING ADVERBS

Adverbs are used to make the meaning of verbs clearer. In the space provided, rewrite each sentence adding an adverb to make the meaning of the verb more exact. Use a different adverb in each sentence. Remember that adverbs answer *when, where, how* or *how much* to the verbs. The verb is underlined and printed in bold type.

1. All day long the rain **pounded** against the window pane.

   _____

   _____

2. At the airport we **watched** the arrivals screen waiting for the plane to land.

   _____

   _____

3. After four days in space the astronauts **jumped** from the space shuttle.

   _____

   _____

4. At the end of the marathon, the first runners **crossed** the finish line.

   _____

   _____

5. The mad scientist **injected** his newly discovered formula into his specimen.

   _____

   _____

6. Even dormant volcanoes **erupt** from time to time.

   _____

   _____

EXERCISE 26: DO NOT CONFUSE ADVERBS AND ADJECTIVES

Adverbs modify verbs; **adjectives** modify nouns. Sometimes writers or speakers incorrectly use adjectives to modify verbs. You have heard someone say, "You did *good*", but *good* is an adjective; the adverb is *well*, so the person should say, "You did *well*."

In this exercise, you will choose either an adjective or an adverb to fit the blank. First discover what the word modifies and then write the correct word in the blank.

1. *good, well*   After I fixed it, my watch worked _____.

2. *slow, slowly*   The jogger ran _____ for the last few blocks.

3. *brave, bravely*   As the brown bear came towards him, the hunter acted _____, staring it down the whole time.

4. *good, well*   Bert did _____ on the test.

5. *good, well*   Bert did _____ work on the test.

6. *loud, loudly*   The waves crashed _____ against the rocks.

7. *careful, carefully*   Drive _____ on the way home.

8. *good, well*   Yolande played _____ the whole game.

9. *quiet, quietly*   The baby slept _____ until noon.

10. *loud, loudly*   The dogs barked _____ at the strangers.

11. *slow, slowly*   Because we were tired, we walked _____ home from the game.

12. *good, well*   Henry is a very _____ writer.

13. *good, well*   Henry writes very _____.

14. *good, well*   This store treats its customers _____.

PART A: THE PARTS OF SPEECH

REVIEW TEST #4: ADVERBS *(20 marks)*

1. Underline the adverb in each of the following sentences. Then draw an arrow to the verb it modifies: (**12 marks**)

   a) Carefully read the question before you attempt to answer it.

   b) The newscaster stopped unexpectedly to read a bulletin.

   c) I will return to school tomorrow after my Christmas vacation.

   d) Kathryn played the game well, so her team won the championship.

   e) The spectators cheered loudly for the home team.

   f) Dinosaurs lived here centuries before human beings arrived.

2. Choose the correct word to fill the blanks in the following sentences. (**8 marks**)

   a) *good, well*   Peter plays soccer very _____.

   b) *good, well*   Peter is a very _____ soccer player.

   c) *slow, slowly*   Time goes by _____ when I am bored.

   d) *quiet, quietly*   The puppy, _____ in its bed, at last gave us some peace.

   e) *brave, bravely*   _____ the soldier walked towards the enemy lines.

   f) *good, well*   Graham plays the accordion _____.

   g) *loud, loudly*   The boxer yelled _____ that he would defeat his opponent.

   h) *good, well*   To get a run, a batter needs to hit the ball _____.

PART A: THE PARTS OF SPEECH

ANSWERS TO EXERCISES ON ADVERBS

Exercise 24: *(page 48)*
1. The little children waited **patiently** for Santa Claus to arrive on Christmas Eve. (***waited***)
2. "I know the answer," the game show contestant shouted **excitedly**. (***shouted***)
3. **Eventually** the rocket rose **steadily** into the sky. (***rose, rose***)
4. The ship sank **instantly** after hitting the iceberg. (***sank***)
5. **Yesterday**, Trudy worked **steadily** on her English exercises. (***worked, worked***)
6. Because Jason plays basketball **well**, he has been selected for the school team. (***plays***)
7. At the recital, Vera danced **gracefully** and the audience applauded **loudly**. (***danced, applauded***)
8. My class went to the museum **today**. (***went***)
9. Thomas read the novel **carefully**, so he was able to answer the questions **accurately**. (***read, answer***)
10. The accident occurred when the car in front of us stopped **unexpectedly**. (***stopped***)
11. The problems of the environment **deeply** concern all human beings. (***concern***)
12. Joe sat **quietly** eating his sandwich. (***sat***)
13. After he went **there**, David developed an interest in California. (***went***)
14. Mother promised she would mail my letter **tomorrow** if she had the time. (***mail***)
15. Ron arrived **promptly** for his interview with Mr. Jones. (***arrived***)
16. Professional athletes train **vigorously** for the upcoming season. (***train***)
17. George **honestly** believed he would see us **later**. (***believed, see***)
18. Susan sat **nervously** waiting for the examination to begin. (***sat***)
19. Sheila walked **elegantly** into the room and took her chair. (***walked***)
20. Bert told the joke **slowly** until he reached the punch-line at the end. (***told***)

Exercise 25: *(page 49)*
Answers may vary.

Exercise 26: *(page 50)*

1. well	2. slowly	3. bravely	4. well	5. good	6. loudly	7. carefully
8. well	9. quietly	10. loudly	11. slowly	12. good	13. well	14. Well

Review Test #4: (page 51)
(1 mark for adverb, 1 mark for verb)
1. a) **carefully** read   b) **unexpectedly** stopped   c) **tomorrow** return   d) **well** played
   e) **loudly** cheered   f) **here** lived
2. a) well   b) good   c) slowly   d) quiet   e) bravely   f) well
   g) loudly   h) well

PART A: THE PARTS OF SPEECH

PREPOSITIONS

What is a Preposition?

A preposition is usually a small word which shows
the relationship of a noun or pronoun
to another word in a sentence.

What are some examples of prepositions?
in, on, under, over, behind, between,
up, upon, through, to, from, with, against.

Why are prepositions important?

A preposition begins a phrase.
A phrase is a group of words;
a prepositional phrase is a group of words beginning with a preposition.

What are some examples of prepositional phrases?
in the book, over the wall, to school, against the wind.

A prepositional phrase always contains a preposition with
a noun or a pronoun.
This noun or pronoun is called the
OBJECT OF THE PREPOSITION.
If you form a question consisting of the preposition and the words
what or *whom*, the answer will always be the object of the preposition.
Example: *in the book*: In what? the book.
Book is the object of the preposition *in.*

PART A: THE PARTS OF SPEECH

EXERCISE 27: IDENTIFYING PREPOSITIONS

Circle the preposition in each of the following sentences.

1. For many years, people have believed that the earth is round.

2. Jeremy took his first trip on an airplane last summer.

3. Niagara Falls is one of the Seven Wonders of the Modern World.

4. My grandfather explained to me that World War II was a vicious war.

5. In the final scene of *Armageddon*, the hero, played by Bruce Willis, dies.

6. After we had lunch at the cottage, we went swimming.

7. After it traveled too quickly around the bend, the car went off the road.

8. The Leaning Tower of Pisa leans so much that people fear it may topple.

9. The policeman opened the door of the bedroom, entered and peered into the closet.

10. Sir Francis Drake was one of the first explorers to sail around the world.

11. The trees in this painting by Tom Thomson appear to have been bent by the wind.

12. Monaco is a tiny principality in southern France, ruled by the Grimaldi family.

13. The fox jumped over the wall and into its hole.

14. Aretha divided the chocolate among her four brothers.

15. Walt stood behind the door to shield himself against the wind.

EXERCISE 28: PREPOSITIONS

In each of the following sentences, circle the preposition which begins a phrase. Underline the object of the preposition in each case.

1. Jeremy took his first trip on an airplane last summer.

2. Niagara Falls is one of the Wonders of the World.

3. My grandfather explained to me that World War II was a vicious war.

4. After it traveled too quickly around the bend, the car went off the road.

5. The Leaning Tower of Pisa leans so much that people fear it may topple.

6. The policeman opened the door of the bedroom, entered and peered into the closet.

7. Sir Francis Drake was one of the first explorers to sail around the world.

8. The trees in this painting by Tom Thomson appear to have been bent by the wind.

9. Monaco is a tiny principality in southern France, ruled by the Grimaldi family.

10. The fox jumped over the wall and into its hole.

11. Aretha divided the chocolate among her four brothers.

12. Walt stood behind the door to shield himself against the wind.

13. *Leavin' on a Jet Plane* was featured in the movie, *Armageddon*.

14. My cousin, Sheila, lives in San Diego.

15. In A Tale of Two Cities, Charles Dickens writes about the French Revolution.

Overhead #21

PREPOSITIONAL PHRASES

Prepositional phrases can work in a sentence as
ADJECTIVE
or
ADVERB.

**If the phrase modifies a noun or pronoun it is a
PREPOSITIONAL ADJECTIVE PHRASE.**

Example:
The man read a quotation from the Bible.
In this sentence, the phrase *from the Bible* modifies the
noun *quotation*. Therefore, it is an adjective phrase.

**If the phrase modifies a verb it is a
PREPOSITIONAL ADVERB PHRASE.**

Example:
We bought the camera on Saturday.
In this sentence, the phrase *on Saturday* modifies the
verb *bought*. Therefore, it is an adverb phrase.

Prepositional phrases then can be either **ADJECTIVE** or **ADVERB.**

EXERCISE 29: PREPOSITIONAL PHRASES

In each of the following sentences, put parentheses ( ) around each prepositional adjective phrase and square brackets [ ] around each prepositional adverb phrase. Draw an arrow from the phrase to the word the phrase modifies.

1. On the Internet a person can find information about many subjects.

2. When Charles married Diana in 1981, the world seemed brighter.

3. Kevin's family came from France and settled in Acadia.

4. The Cajuns of Louisiana are the descendents of the original settlers of Acadia.

5. When Peter visited New Orleans he bought a voodoo doll at a little shop.

6. The Olympics were held twice in Lake Placid.

7. When Rembrandt lived in Holland, he painted many portraits of Dutch people.

8. Walt Disney's *Bambi* turned many people against hunting.

9. A good government works for the people.

10. In the cement outside Mann's Chinese Theater, people can see the footprints of stars such as Marilyn Monroe and Shirley Temple.

11. Corin comes from Sri Lanka, a country once called Ceylon.

12. Zidane was a valuable player for France in the World Cup.

13. Renée rode her horse over the jumps and through the trotting poles.

14. Jacques Villeneuve, the son of Gilles Villeneuve, is a famous Grand Prix driver.

15. The Tansley family lives just around the corner.

PART A: THE PARTS OF SPEECH

REVIEW TEST #5: PREPOSITIONS AND PHRASES (*20 marks*)

For each of the following sentences:

- circle the preposition
- underline the object of the preposition
- put parentheses ( ) around adjective phrases or square brackets [ ] around adverb phrases
- draw an arrow from the phrase to the word it modifies.

Example: When the north poles (of two **magnets**) are brought together, they repel.

1. Jamie was born in 1992.

2. Chocolate is made from the cocoa bean.

3. I entered my house through the back door.

4. The length of a year is 365 days.

5. Otis wanted to sit at the back.

PART A: THE PARTS OF SPEECH

ANSWERS TO EXERCISES ON PREPOSITIONS

Exercise 27: *(page 54)*

1. for	**2.** on	**3.** of, of	**4.** to	**5.** in	**6.** at
7. around, off	**8.** of	**9.** of, into	**10.** of	**11.** in, by, by	**12.** in, by
13. over, into	**14.** among	**15.** behind, against			

Exercise 28: *(page 55)*

The preposition to be circled is listed in parentheses after the sentence.

1. Jeremy took his first trip on an **airplane** last summer. (**on**)
2. Niagara Falls is one of the **Wonders** of the **World**. (**of, of**)
3. My grandfather explained to **me** that World War II was a vicious war. (**to**)
4. After it traveled too quickly around the **bend**, the car went off the **road**. (**around, off**)
5. The Leaning Tower of **Pisa** leans so much that people fear it may topple. (**of**)
6. The policeman opened the door of the **bedroom**, entered and peered into the **closet**. (**of, into**)
7. Sir Francis Drake was one of the first **explorers** to sail around the **world**. (**of, around**)
8. The trees in this **painting** by **Tom Thomson** appear to have been bent by the <u>wind</u>. (**in, by, by**)
9. Monaco is a tiny principality in southern **France**, ruled by the **Grimaldi family**. (**in, by**): *Note: <u>family</u> is acceptable.*
10. The fox jumped over the **wall** and into its **hole**. (**over, into**)
11. Aretha divided the chocolate among her four **brothers**. (**among**)
12. Walt stood behind the **door** to shield himself against the **wind**. (**behind, against**)
13. *Leavin' on a **Jet Plane*** was featured in the **movie**, *Armageddon*. (**on, in**)
14. My cousin, Sheila, lives in **San Diego**. (**in**)
15. In **A Tale of Two Cities**, Charles Dickens writes about the **French Revolution**. (**in, about**)

Exercise 29: *(page 57)*

Word the phrase modifies is after dash at end of sentence.

1. [On the Internet] a person can find information [about many subjects]. – *can find, can find*
2. When Charles married Diana [in 1981], the world seemed brighter. – *married*
3. Kevin's family came [from France] and settled [in Acadia]. – *came, settled*
4. The Cajuns (of Louisiana) are the descendents (of the original settlers) (of Acadia). – *Cajuns, descendents, settlers*
5. When Peter visited New Orleans he bought a voodoo doll [at a little shop]. – *bought*
6. The Olympics were held twice [in Lake Placid]. – *were held*
7. When Rembrandt lived [in Holland], he painted many portraits (of Dutch people). – *lived, portraits*
8. Walt Disney's *Bambi* turned many people [against hunting]. – *turned*
9. A good government works [for the people]. – *works*
10. [In the cement] [outside Mann's Chinese Theater], people can see the footprints (of stars) such as **Marilyn Monroe and Shirley Temple.** – *can see, can see, footprints*
11. Corin comes [from Sri Lanka], a country once called Ceylon. – *comes*
12. Zidane was a valuable player (for France) (in the World Cup). – *player, player*
13. Renée rode her horse [over the jumps] and [through the trotting poles]. – *rode, rode*
14. Jacques Villeneuve, the son (of Gilles Villeneuve), is a famous Grand Prix driver. – *son*
15. The Tansley family lives just [around the corner]. – *lives*

Review Test#5: *(page 58)*

1. Jamie was born [(in) 1992].
2. Chocolate is made [(from) the **cocoa bean**]. *Bean alone is fine.*
3. I entered my house [(through) the **back door**]. *Door alone is fine.*
4. The length ((of) a **year**) is 365 days.
5. Otis wanted to sit [(at) the **back**].

PART A: THE PARTS OF SPEECH

Overhead #22

CONJUNCTIONS

The word *conjunction* comes from two Latin words:
CON means *with* or *together with*
and
JUNGO means *I join*.

Therefore a conjunction is a joining word.

There are two types of conjunctions:

1. CO-ORDINATE CONJUNCTIONS

are words that join two other words, phrases or sentences
of equal value.

There are only seven co-ordinate conjunctions in English:
and, *but*, *or*, *nor*, *for*, *yet* and *so*.

2. SUBORDINATE CONJUNCTIONS

are words that join a sentence to another sentence.

Here are some examples of subordinate conjunctions:
if, *because*, *until*, *when*, *although*, *since*.

EXERCISE 30: CONJUNCTIONS

In each of the following sentences, circle each conjunction. Then in the blank space provided, identify the conjunction as co-ordinate or subordinate. (Remember that there are only seven co-ordinate conjunctions.)

1. Last Christmas, I bought gifts for both my sister and my brother. _____

2. Carole did not go to school today because she had the flu. _____

3. Rita wanted to become a doctor, but she did not have enough money to attend medical school. _____

4. Although Mark McGwire broke the record first, Sammy Sosa was not far behind. _____

5. The northernmost regions of Europe, North America and Asia bordering on the Arctic Circle are called the *tundra*. _____

6. Marissa's grandfather wanted to buy a CD by the Beatles or the Rolling Stones. _____

7. The Greeks were probably the first people to make coins and use them as money. _____

8. Many people speak English, but Mandarin is the most spoken language in the world. _____

9. If you brush your teeth every day, you should be able to keep your teeth healthy. _____

10. Irving had never read a book by Mark Twain until he read <u>Huckleberry Finn</u>. _____

PART A: THE PARTS OF SPEECH

INTERJECTIONS

The word *interjection* comes from two Latin words:
INTER means *between* and *JACERE* means *to throw*.

Therefore an interjection is simply a word or phrase
thrown into a sentence.

Here are some examples of interjections:

well
alas
goodbye
hello
Oh
my goodness
Ouch!
Wow!
Yippee!
Ugh!

Note that these words often express strong emotion.

**Interjections have NO GRAMMATICAL FUNCTION
in a sentence
and therefore are
the least important of the parts of speech.**

Overhead #24

AVOID UNNECESSARY INTERJECTIONS

PART A: THE PARTS OF SPEECH

EXERCISE 31: INTERJECTIONS

Circle the interjections in the following sentences.

1. Well, I said I thought he should be able to go to Montana next summer.

2. Yippee! I can really go to Montana?

3. I discovered, alas, that I had made the wrong decision.

4. "Like--oh, my God, Wow!" interjected the inarticulate speaker.

5. My goodness! That was an awful thing to do!

EXERCISE 32: INTERJECTIONS

Rewrite each of the following sentences, adding an interjection which might be appropriate to the meaning of the sentence.

1. You said I really won the contest?

   _____

2. This is Erica Saunders speaking.

   _____

3. That mosquito really bit me hard.

   _____

4. I didn't see you there.

   _____

5. I really hate doing exercises on interjections.

   _____

PART A: THE PARTS OF SPEECH

ANSWERS TO EXERCISES ON CONJUNCTIONS AND INTERJECTIONS

Exercise 30: *(page 61)*
1. and - co-ordinate
2. because - subordinate
3. but - co-ordinate
4. although - subordinate
5. and - co-ordinate
6. or - co-ordinate
7. and - co-ordinate
8. but - co-ordinate
9. if - subordinate
10. until - subordinate

Exercise 31: *(page 63)*
1. well
2. yippee
3. alas
4. like, oh, my God, Wow
5. my goodness.

Exercise 32: *(page 63)*
Answers may vary.

PART B: THE PARTS OF THE SENTENCE

Overhead #25

> # THE SENTENCE

What is a Sentence?

> **A sentence is a group of words which expresses a complete thought.**

Normally, the complete thought in a sentence is expressed through

> # SUBJECT AND PREDICATE

What is a Subject?

> **A SUBJECT is a single word or group of words which tells what (or whom) the sentence is about. A subject is normally the most important noun or pronoun in the sentence.**

What are some examples of subjects in sentences?

Gareth **took the train to London on Saturday.**

The players on the football team **celebrated their victory.**

Many Canadians living overseas **help people in other countries.**

PART B: THE PARTS OF THE SENTENCE

EXERCISE 33: IDENTIFYING SUBJECTS

Underline the complete subject in each of the following sentences.

1. Many people go to the movies on weekends.

2. Shannon was the first person to see my new puppy.

3. Guernsey, an island in the English Channel, was occupied during World War II.

4. Bugs Bunny and Daffy Duck have both appeared on stamps in the United States.

5. My father's favorite movie is *Casablanca*, starring Humphrey Bogart.

6. Wyatt Earp and his brothers fought in the famous gunfight at the O.K. Corral.

7. Hong Kong was returned to China in 1997.

8. You must win the qualifying round in order to advance in play.

9. French people consider Napoleon among their greatest leaders.

10. The teacher gave us five pages of homework in Science.

11. Mrs. Brown works for a fashion magazine.

12. Aunt Pauline traveled to Australia, New Zealand and Fiji last summer.

13. The photograph shows my grandfather with a baby on his lap.

14. Theresa and Elizabeth are coming to my house for dinner tonight.

15. Cabbage rolls are among the most delicious foods from Poland.

16. Sam McLaughlin's carriage factory in Oshawa became part of General Motors of Canada.

17. January was the coldest month on record.

18. Ernest Hemingway set his novel, The Old Man and the Sea, in Cuba.

19. Erica and her friends went skating last Friday.

20. A sentence is a group of words which express a complete thought.

PART B: THE PARTS OF THE SENTENCE

SUBJECT AND PREDICATE

Remember that a subject tells what the sentence is about.

The **PREDICATE** tells something about the subject,
usually what the subject is doing.

What are some examples of predicates in sentences?

Gareth *took the train to London on Saturday.*

The players on the football team *celebrated their victory.*

Many Amercians living overseas *help people in other countries.*

Note that in these examples the entire sentence is divided into
Complete Subject
and
Complete Predicate.
There are no words left over.

PART B: THE PARTS OF THE SENTENCE

EXERCISE 34: IDENTIFYING SUBJECTS AND PREDICATES

Draw a vertical line between the complete subject and complete predicate in each of the following sentences. Then underline the complete subject with a single line and the complete predicate with a double line.

Example: <u>Many people</u> | <u>go to the movies on weekends</u>.

1. Birds often make their nests in the trees in our backyard.

2. The Year of the Tiger was celebrated in 1998.

3. Little Nell is a popular character in *The Old Curiosity Shop* by Charles Dickens.

4. The capital of Mexico is Mexico City.

5. Mother's Day is the second Sunday in May.

6. Frozen packaged food was invented by Clarence Birdseye in 1924.

7. Clarence Birdseye invented frozen packaged food in 1924.

8. The space shuttle, *Challenger*, exploded 73 seconds after takeoff.

9. Sound waves can travel through air, water, wood and other materials.

10. One of the best-selling games of the twentieth century is *Monopoly*.

11. *Monopoly* is one of the best-selling games of the twentieth century.

12. Vatican City is the smallest country in the world in area.

13. The smallest country in the world in population is Vatican City.

14. Dr. James Naismith invented the game of basketball.

PART B: THE PARTS OF THE SENTENCE
ANSWERS TO EXERCISES ON SUBJECT AND PREDICATE

Exercise 33: *(page 67)*
1. **Many people** go to the movies on weekends.
2. **Shannon** was the first person to see my new puppy.
3. **Guernsey, an island in the English Channel**, was occupied during World War II.
4. **Bugs Bunny and Daffy Duck** have both appeared on stamps from the United States.
5. **My father's favorite movie** is *Casablanca*, starring Humphrey Bogart.
6. **Wyatt Earp and his brothers** fought in the famous gunfight at the O.K. Corral.
7. **Hong Kong** was returned to China in 1997.
8. **You** must win the qualifying round in order to advance in play.
9. **French people** consider Napoleon among their greatest leaders.
10. **The teacher** gave us five pages of homework in Science.
11. **Mrs. Brown** works for a fashion magazine.
12. **Aunt Pauline** traveled to Australia, New Zealand and Fiji last summer.
13. **The photograph** shows my grandfather with a baby on his lap.
14. **Theresa and Elizabeth** are coming to my house for dinner tonight.
15. **Cabbage rolls** are among the most delicious foods from Poland.
16. **Sam McLaughlin's carriage factory in Oshawa** became part of General Motors of Canada.
17. **January** was the coldest month on record.
18. **Ernest Hemingway** set his novel, The Old Man and the Sea, in Cuba.
19. **Erica and her friends** went skating last Friday.
20. **A sentence** is a group of words which express a complete thought.

Exercise 34: (page 69)
1. Birds | often make their nests in the trees in our backyard.
2. The Year of the Tiger | was celebrated in 1998.
3. Little Nell | is a popular character in *The Old Curiosity Shop* by Charles Dickens.
4. The capital of Mexico | is Mexico City.
5. Mother's Day | is the second Sunday in May.
6. Frozen packaged food | was invented by Clarence Birdseye in 1924.
7. Clarence Birdseye | invented frozen packaged food in 1924.
8. The space shuttle, *Challenger*, | exploded seventy-three seconds after takeoff.
9. Sound waves | can travel through air, water, wood and other materials.
10. One of the best-selling games of the twentieth century | is *Monopoly*.
11. *Monopoly* | is one of the best-selling games of the twentieth century.
12. Vatican City | is the smallest country in the world in area.
13. The smallest country in the world in population | is Vatican City.
14. Dr. James Naismith | invented the game of basketball.

PART B: THE PARTS OF THE SENTENCE

BARE SUBJECT AND BARE PREDICATE

The **BARE SUBJECT** is the noun or pronoun which is
the focus of the sentence.
Normally it is the doer of the action in the sentence.
The complete subject consists of:
the bare subject and its modifiers.

Example of a bare subject with its modifiers:

A small *girl* approached the microphone.
The complete subject is *A small girl*, but the words
a and *small* are modifiers of the bare subject *girl*.

The **BARE PREDICATE** is simply the verb in the sentence--
but it is the complete verb.

Example: Roger *is working* on the farm this summer.

Note that the complete predicate is *is working on the farm this summer.*
On the farm and *this summer* are modifiers of the bare predicate
is working.

EXERCISE 35: IDENTIFYING SUBJECTS AND PREDICATES

Draw a vertical line between the complete subject and complete predicate in each of the following sentences. Then underline the bare subject with a single line and the bare predicate with a double line.

1. Edward Lear was a writer of nonsense poetry.

2. He was born in London, England, in 1812.

3. In his youth, he painted many pictures, especially of birds.

4. Lord Stanley hired Lear to draw the animals in his private zoo.

5. Lear began also to draw pictures for Lord Stanley's children.

6. He also wrote nonsense rhymes for the pictures.

7. In 1846, Lear published <u>A Book of Nonsense</u>.

8. The book became very popular.

9. He then wrote more nonsense poetry.

10. These nonsense poems were published in later books.

11. Lear's most famous poem is called "The Owl and the Pussycat".

12. The limerick, a five-lined humorous poem, was invented by Edward Lear.

13. Edward Lear died in San Remo, Italy, in 1870.

PART B: THE PARTS OF THE SENTENCE

Overhead #28

COMPOUND SUBJECTS

Two or more nouns or pronouns may be used as the subject
in a sentence.
This is called a Compound Subject.

What are some examples of Compound Subjects?

Two nouns: *Zachary* and *Henry* went to the movies.
In this sentence, two nouns comprise the subject,
but there is only one verb, *went*.

Two pronouns: *She* and *I* went to the movies.
In this sentence, two pronouns comprise the subject,
but there is only one verb, *went*.

One noun and one pronoun: *Mary* and *I* went to the movies.
In this sentence, one noun (*Mary*) and one pronoun (*I*)
comprise the subject.

Note that a compound subject is plural, as is a
single plural subject.
Example: *Two friends* went to the movies.

EXERCISE 36: COMPOUND SUBJECTS

Underline the subject with a single line in each of the following sentences. Look out for compound subjects and underline both of them. Not all sentences contain compound subjects.

1. <u>Huckleberry Finn</u> is the story of a young boy living during the days of slavery.

2. Huck makes friends with a runaway slave, named Jim.

3. In order to find freedom, Huck and Jim sail a raft down the Mississippi River.

4. Along the way, they meet many strange and curious people.

5. The Grangerfords and the Shepherdsons are two families involved in a feud.

6. The King and the Duke are con-men trying to swindle any foolish people.

7. Mary Jane, Susan and Joanna Wilks are among the King and the Duke's victims.

8. Huck runs into Tom Sawyer at the Phelps farm.

9. Uncle Silas and Aunt Sally are Tom's relatives.

10. Uncle Silas locks up Jim, thinking he is a runaway slave.

11. Through the last part of the story, Huck and Tom try to free Jim.

12. <u>Huckleberry Finn</u> and <u>Tom Sawyer</u> are two different books written by Mark Twain.

13. Both Huck and Tom are characters in both books.

Overhead #29

COMPOUND PREDICATES

Two or more verbs may be used as the predicate
in a sentence.
This is called a Compound Predicate.

What are some examples of Compound Predicates?

I *walked* to the arena and then *went* skating.

My money *might have been lost* or *might have been stolen*.

The bull *snorted* and *came* towards me.

**Compound Predicates and Compound Subjects
can exist in the same sentence.**

Examples: <u>Rory</u> and <u>Delilah</u> <u>visited</u> me earlier and <u>went</u> home.

<u>My sister</u> and <u>I</u> <u>did</u> our chores and then <u>slept</u>.

EXERCISE 37: COMPOUND SUBJECTS AND PREDICATES

In each of the following sentences, underline the subject with a single line and the verb (simple predicate) with a double line. Look out for compound subjects and predicates to make sure you underline both of them. Not all sentences contain compound subjects and predicates.

1. Charlestown is the capital city of Nevis, an island in the Caribbean.

2. Not many people live in Charlestown.

3. However, the local residents are both happy and friendly people.

4. Charlestown is a seaport and a commercial center.

5. The pier was built in the harbor, just a few steps from any building in town.

6. The ferryboat makes several crossings each day to the sister island of St. Kitts.

7. St. Kitts and Nevis are joined in government and so have become one country.

8. Many people from Nevis have relatives in St. Kitts and visit them often.

9. Both islands are little pieces of Paradise and welcome tourists.

PART B: THE PARTS OF A SENTENCE

REVIEW TEST #6: SUBJECT AND PREDICATE (20 marks)

For each of the following sentences, underline the bare subject with one line and the bare predicate with two lines. Watch out for compound subjects or predicates.

1. Galileo did many experiments at the Leaning Tower of Pisa.

2. In the first chapter, Maury and Dennis discover a secret cave.

3. My aunt draws pictures and colors them well.

4. The boys on Helen's hockey team respect her skills in the game.

5. Stubborn people often get their own way.

6. Many children like to spend their time playing video games.

7. Kingston and Niagara-on-the-Lake were once capitals of Canada.

8. Abraham Lincoln freed the slaves in 1861.

9. Marvin played well and scored two goals.

10. Ancient Romans conquered much of Europe.

PART B: THE PARTS OF THE SENTENCE
ANSWERS TO EXERCISES ON SUBJECT AND PREDICATE

Exercise 35: *(page 72)*

1. **Edward Lear** | **was** a writer of nonsense poetry.
2. **He** | **was born** in London, England, in 1812.
3. In his youth, **he** | **painted** many pictures, especially of birds.
4. **Lord Stanley** | **hired** Lear to draw the animals in his private zoo.
5. **Lear** | **began** also to draw pictures for Lord Stanley's children.
6. **He** | also **wrote** nonsense rhymes for the pictures.
7. In 1846, **Lear** | **published** A Book of Nonsense.
8. The **book** | **became** very popular.
9. **He** | then **wrote** more nonsense poetry.
10. These nonsense **poems** | **were published** in later books.
11. Lear's most famous **poem** | **is called** "The Owl and the Pussycat".
12. The **limerick**, a five-lined humorous poem, | **was invented** by Edward Lear.
13. **Edward Lear** | **died** in San Remo, Italy, in 1870.

Exercise 36: *(page 74)*
The subjects only are listed:

1. Huckleberry Finn   2. Huck   3. Huck, Jim   4. they   5. Grangerfords, Shepherdsons
6. King, Duke   7. Mary Jane, Susan, Joanna Wilks   8. Huck
9. Uncle Silas, Aunt Sally   10. Uncle Silas   11. Huck, Tom
12. Huckleberry Finn, Tom Sawyer   13. Huck, Tom.

Exercise 37: *(page 76)*

1. **Charlestown is** the capital city of Nevis, an island in the Caribbean.
2. Not many **people live** in Charlestown.
3. However, the local **residents are** both happy and friendly people.
4. **Charlestown is** a seaport and a commercial center.
5. The **pier was built** in the harbor, just a few steps from any building in town.
6. The **ferryboat makes** several crossings each day to the sister island of St. Kitts.
7. **St. Kitts** and **Nevis are joined** in government and so **have become** one country.
8. Many **people** from Nevis **have** relatives in St. Kitts and **visit** them often.
9. Both **islands are** little pieces of Paradise and **welcome** tourists.

Review Test #6: *(page 77)*

1. **Galileo did** many experiments at the Leaning Tower of Pisa.
2. In the first chapter, **Maury** and **Dennis discover** a secret cave.
3. My **aunt draws** pictures and **colors** them well.
4. The **boys** on Helen's hockey team **respect** her skills in the game.
5. Stubborn **people** often **get** their own way.
6. Many **children** like to **spend** their **time playing** video games.
7. **Kingston** and **Niagara-on-the-Lake were** once capitals of Canada.
8. **Abraham Lincoln freed** the slaves in 1861. (*Lincoln, by itself, is acceptable.*)
9. **Marvin played** well and **scored** two goals.
10. Ancient **Romans conquered** much of Europe.

Overhead #30

PRINCIPAL CLAUSES

What is the difference between a Phrase and a Clause?

A PHRASE is a group of words.

A CLAUSE is a group of words which contains a subject and a verb.

All sentences are made up of one or more clauses.

A PRINCIPAL CLAUSE is the part of the sentence

which expresses a complete thought.

It can stand alone as a sentence.

Principal Clauses are also called:

- Independent Clauses or
  - Main Clauses.

Example of a Principal Clause:

Ryan answered the teacher's question.

In this sentence, the subject is *Ryan* and the verb is *answered*.

The sentence makes complete sense by itself.

Now look at this group of words:

Ryan answering the teacher's question.

This sentence does not have a complete verb,

so it does not make sense by itself:

It needs other words to complete it.

Because I was late.

This group of words has a subject and a verb but it does not make sense by

itself; it is not a Principal Clause.

EXERCISE 38: IDENTIFYING PRINCIPAL CLAUSES

Identify the underlined group of words in the following sentences, by writing **PHRASE** or **PRINCIPAL CLAUSE** in the blank provided. Remember that prepositional phrases begin with a preposition, but a phrase generally is a group of words.

1. When he visited New York, <u>Ethan saw the Statue of Liberty</u>. _____

2. When he visited New York, Ethan saw the Statue <u>of Liberty</u>. _____

3. <u>While in New York</u>, Ethan saw the Statue of Liberty. _____

4. <u>Subordinate clauses cannot stand alone</u>. _____

5. Dorothy walked <u>to the park</u> after school. _____

6. Dorothy walked to the park <u>after school</u>. _____

7. <u>Dorothy walked to the park after school</u>. _____

8. William Shakespeare attended <u>Stratford Grammar School</u>. _____

9. <u>William Shakespeare attended Stratford Grammar School</u>. _____

10. <u>Because of my lateness</u>, I had to stay in after school. _____

11. Because of my lateness, <u>I had to stay in after school</u>. _____

12. Because of my lateness, I had to stay in <u>after school</u>. _____

13. <u>The computer science field attracts many people every year</u>. _____

14. The computer science field attracts many people <u>every year</u>. _____

15. <u>The computer science field</u> attracts many people every year. _____

16. <u>Tropical rainforests are found along the Amazon</u> in Brazil. _____

17. Tropical rainforests are found <u>along the Amazon</u> in Brazil. _____

18. Tropical rainforests are found along the Amazon <u>in Brazil</u>. _____

19. <u>Tropical rainforests are found</u> along the Amazon <u>in Brazil</u>. _____

20. In Michigan it was once illegal <u>to hitch a crocodile to a fire hydrant</u>. _____

21. <u>In Michigan</u> it was once illegal to hitch a crocodile to a fire hydrant. _____

22. In Michigan <u>it was once illegal to hitch a crocodile to a fire hydrant</u>. _____

PART B: THE PARTS OF THE SENTENCE

Overhead #31

SUBORDINATE CLAUSES

Remember that a Principal Clause is like a sentence:
It makes complete sense by itself and can stand alone.

A SUBORDINATE CLAUSE
also has a subject and a verb
but it cannot stand alone.
It needs a Principal Clause in order to make complete sense.
For this reason, it is sometimes called a Dependent Clause,
because it <u>depends</u> on the Principal Clause.

Examples of Subordinate Clauses:
1. since it was on the table
2. when I grow up
3. because I tried.

Notice that these sentences make complete sense with a Principal Clause.
1. Since it was on the table, I ate the piece of pie.
2. I want to be a doctor when I grow up.
3. Because I tried, I did well at the team tryouts.

Note that Subordinate Clauses may be placed in front of or after the
Principal Clause:
1. I ate the piece of pie since it was on the table.
2. When I grow up, I want to be a doctor.
3. I did well at the team tryouts because I tried.
Yes, you *can* start a sentence with *because*—if you finish the sentence
with a Principal Clause.

EXERCISE 39: IDENTIFYING SUBORDINATE CLAUSES

In the blank space provided tell whether the underlined group of words is a **PRINCIPAL CLAUSE**, a **SUBORDINATE CLAUSE** or a **PHRASE**.

1. <u>When he went to the zoo</u>, Daniel saw the lions and bears. _____

2. When he went to the zoo, <u>Daniel saw the lions and bears</u>. _____

3. When he went <u>to the zoo</u>, Daniel saw the lions and bears. _____

4. Aline read her speech to the class <u>on Wednesday</u>. _____

5. <u>Aline read her speech to the class</u> on Wednesday. _____

6. Aline read her speech <u>to the class</u> on Wednesday. _____

7. <u>Cactus plants grow in deserts</u> where it does not rain much. _____

8. Cactus plants grow in deserts <u>where it does not rain much</u>. _____

9. Cactus plants grow <u>in deserts</u> where it does not rain much. _____

10. <u>When she goes to the Museum</u>, Tara sees the fossils. _____

11. When she goes <u>to the Museum</u>, Tara sees the fossils. _____

12. When she goes to the Museum, <u>Tara sees the fossils</u>. _____

13. <u>After a snowfall</u>, the world looks like a painting. _____

14. After a snowfall, <u>the world looks like a painting</u>. _____

15. After a snowfall, the world looks <u>like a painting</u>. _____

16. <u>After I finish my homework</u>, I am allowed to watch TV. _____

17. After I finish my homework, <u>I am allowed to watch TV</u>. _____

18. <u>If you work hard</u>, you will be promoted in this company. _____

19. If you work hard, <u>you will be promoted</u> in this company. _____

20. If you work hard, you will be promoted <u>in this company</u>. _____

21. <u>Firefighters risk their lives</u> every day to save others. _____

22. <u>Firefighters risk their lives every day</u> to save others. _____

23. Firefighters risk their lives <u>every day</u> to save others. _____

24. <u>I like principal clauses</u>. _____

Overhead #32

KINDS OF SUBORDINATE CLAUSES

There are three kinds of Subordinate Clauses:
- Subordinate Adjective Clauses work like single adjectives:
They modify nouns or pronouns.
- Subordinate Noun Clauses work like single nouns:
They are used as subject, object or subjective completion.
- Subordinate Adverb Clauses work like single adverbs:
They modify verbs, adjectives or other adverbs.

1. SUBORDINATE ADJECTIVE CLAUSES
generally begin with a Relative Pronoun.
The Relative Pronouns are: *who, whom, whose, that, which.*
Example: Joanne, *who is in my class*, is an excellent student.
In this sentence, the Relative Pronoun *who* introduces the Subordinate
Adjective Clause *who is in my class* which modifies the noun *Joanne.*

2. SUBORDINATE NOUN CLAUSES
are usually introduced by *that, what, whatever, who, whoever, whom.*
Note that many of these words are the same as those listed to begin
Subordinate Adjective Clauses.
However, the Subordinate Noun Clause functions as a noun in a sentence;
that is, is can be subject, object or subjective completion.
Example: *Whatever you say* is fine with me.
In this sentence, *whatever you say* functions as the subject.
Therefore, this is a Subordinate Noun Clause.

KINDS OF SUBORDINATE CLAUSES
(Continued)

3. SUBORDINATE ADVERB CLAUSES

answer the questions *when, where, why, how, how much.*
They are introduced by SUBORDINATE CONJUNCTIONS.
The following chart lists the most important Subordinate Conjunctions:

after	before	unless
although	if	until
as	since	when
as long as	so that	whenever
as soon as	than	where
because	though	while

Examples:

1. *Because Stephanie went out,* she missed Marnie's visit.

In this sentence, *because Stephanie went out* answers the question
why to the verb *missed.*
Therefore it is a Subordinate Adverb Clause.

2. Herman waited *until Gretchen got home.*

In this sentence, *until Gretchen got home* answers the question
when to the verb *waited.*
It too is a Subordinate Adverb Clause.

PART B: THE PARTS OF THE SENTENCE

EXERCISE 40: IDENTIFYING SUBORDINATE CLAUSES

For each of these sentences, do the following:

a) Underline the subject of the principal clause with a single line. If a noun clause is used as subject, underline the entire noun clause.

b) Underline the verb in the principal clause with a double line.

c) Put parentheses ( ) around each subordinate adjective clause and draw an arrow to the noun or pronoun which it modifies.

d) Put brackets [ ] around each subordinate adverb clause and draw an arrow to the verb it modifies.

1. When students in the class are speaking, other students should listen quietly.

2. What I like at the circus are the clowns and the acrobats.

3. Gaston knew why he had won the award for top student.

4. Paris is the city where I was born.

5. A girl who lives in Florida taught her pet alligator to sing.

6. Whoever sent you those flowers is a great admirer.

7. When she saw *Armageddon* Olivia wanted to see it again and again.

8. What a person values in life is important to those around him.

9. Jim finishes his homework before he watches television.

10. Lyda travels to France often because her sister lives there.

11. Unless my mother changes her mind, I will not be going to Boston this spring.

12. A stranger, who looked a little like Tom Cruise, came to my table.

13. Before she plays soccer, Leah does warm-up exercises.

14. Scientists who study the stars are called astronomers.

15. Zeus, who was the King of the Gods in Greek mythology, married Hera.

PART B: THE PARTS OF THE SENTENCE

EXERCISE 41: SENTENCE FRAGMENTS

In the blanks provided, write a complete sentence from each subordinate clause which follows. In some cases, you may make the subordinate clause into a principal clause, but in others you should add a principal clause to it.

1. although I am not a detective _____

_____

2. that Howie would win the prize _____

_____

3. after you beat the eggs _____

_____

4. because Meredith was late for dancing lessons _____

_____

5. if I won a lottery _____

_____

6. who lives in Tasmania _____

_____

7. after Queen Elizabeth executed the Earl of Essex _____

_____

8. before we see each other again _____

_____

9. who lived in Arizona for five years _____

_____

REVIEW TEST #7: CLAUSES (20 marks)

A) Underline the principal clause in each of the following sentences: (**6 marks**)

1. Dad went to the store because he needed more garlic for his Caesarsalad.

2. Before I knew Uncle Albert, he sent me many presents for my birthday.

3. A stitch in time saves nine.

4. My little brother, who has always been a pest, was on his worst behavior.

5. Jonathon always works very hard in class.

6. The *Wright Brothers* sold bicycles before they invented the airplane.

B) Underline the subordinate clause in each of the following sentences. In the blank space provided, state whether the subordinate clause works as noun, adjective or adverb. (**14 marks**)

1. When Maggie goes to soccer games, she cheers for the team. _____

2. I do my homework until I go to bed. _____

3. Whatever you say will be fine. _____

4. Shannon was elected captain because she works very hard. _____

5. Peter wrote to Caroline, who lives in Guatemala. _____

6. Bella wears a hat which she bought at the fair. _____

7. Before I read a book, I find a nice comfy chair. _____

PART B: THE PARTS OF THE SENTENCE
ANSWERS TO EXERCISES ON CLAUSES

Exercise 38: *(page 80)*

1. principal clause	**2.** phrase	**3.** phrase	**4.** principal clause	**5.** phrase
6. phrase	**7.** principal clause	**8.** phrase	**9.** principal clause	**10.** phrase
11. principal clause	**12.** phrase	**13.** principal clause	**14.** phrase	**15.** phrase
16. principal clause	**17.** phrase	**18.** phrase	**19.** principal clause	**20.** phrase
21. phrase	**22.** principal clause			

Exercise 39: *(page 82)*

1. subordinate clause	**2.** principal clause	**3.** phrase	**4.** phrase
5. principal clause	**6.** phrase	**7.** principal clause	**8.** subordinate clause
9. phrase	**10.** subordinate clause	**11.** phrase	**12.** principal claus
13. phrase	**14.** principal clause	**15.** phrase	**16.** subordinate clause
17. principal clause	**18.** subordinate clause	**19.** principal clause	**20.** phrase
21. principal clause	**22.** principal clause	**23.** phrase	**24.** principal clause

Exercise 40: *(page 85)*

1. [When students in the class are speaking,] other **students should listen** quietly.
2. **What I like at the circus are** the clowns and the acrobats.
3. **Gaston knew** [why he had won the award for top student].
4. **Paris is** the city (where I was born).
5. A **girl** (who lives in Florida) **taught** her pet alligator to sing.
6. **Whoever sent you those flowers is** a great admirer.
7. [When she saw *Armageddon*] **Olivia wanted** to see it again and again.
8. **What a person values in life is** important to those around him.
9. **Jim finishes** his homework [before he watches television].
10. **Lyda travels** to France often [because her sister lives there].
11. [Unless my mother changes her mind,] **I will** not **be going** to Boston this spring.
12. A **stranger**, (who looked a little like Tom Cruise,) **came** to my table.
13. [Before she plays soccer,] **Leah does** warm-up exercises.
14. **Scientists** (who study the stars) **are called** astronomers.
15. **Zeus**, (who was the King of the Gods in Greek mythology,) **married** Hera.

Review Test #7: *(page 87)*

A)
1. **Dad went to the store** because he needed more garlic for his Caesar salad.
2. Before I knew Uncle Albert, **he sent me many presents for my birthday**.
3. **A stitch in time saves nine**.
4. **My little brother**, who has always been a pest, **was on his worst behavior**.
5. **Jonathon always works very hard in class**.
6. **The Wright Brothers sold bicycles** before they invented the airplane.

B)
1. **When Maggie goes to soccer games**, she cheers for the team. - **adverb**
2. I do my homework **until I go to bed**. - **adverb**
3. **Whatever you say** will be fine. - **noun**
4. Shannon was elected captain **because she works very hard**. - **adverb**
5. Peter wrote to Caroline, **who lives in Guatemala**. - **adjective**
6. Bella wears a hat **which she bought at the fair**. - **adjective**
7. **Before I read a book**, I find a nice comfy chair. - **adverb**

Overhead #34

KINDS OF SENTENCES

When we combine principal and subordinate clauses to form sentences we can create four kinds of sentences.
Here are three of them:

1. **SIMPLE SENTENCES** consist of one principal clause.
Example: *Joan went to school.*
Notice that simple sentences may be long or short:
The soldiers entered the village.
After struggling with the wintery weather in the trenches, the soldiers wearily entered the village, happy to see other people.
In spite of all the words in this sentence, it still contains one principal clause along with its modifiers.

2. **COMPOUND SENTENCES** consist of two or more principal clauses.
Example: *Marla played baseball and Joshua watched television.*
This sentence consists of two principal clauses, each of which is a complete sentence by itself.
Marla played baseball. Joshua watched television.

3. **COMPLEX SENTENCES** consist of one principal clause and one or more subordinate clauses.
Example: *Marla played baseball while Joshua watched television.*
While Joshua watched television is a subordinate adverb clause which answers the question *when* to *played.*
The writer puts the less important idea into the subordinate clause.
So this sentence emphasizes Marla playing baseball.
Joshua watched television while Marla played baseball
places the emphasis on Joshua rather than Marla.

PART B: THE PARTS OF THE SENTENCE

EXERCISE 42: IDENTIFYING KINDS OF SENTENCES

In the space provided, identify the kind of sentence as **simple**, **compound**, or **complex**.

1. Harvester ants live in deserts and feed mainly on seeds. _____

2. A roadrunner crushes lizards and snakes with its strong feet before it eats them. _____

3. Sand cats live in deserts in North Africa and Arabia. _____

4. The yellow-brown fur of the sand cat helps to camouflage it against the sand as it stalks its prey. _____

5. A kangaroo rat looks like a tiny kangaroo as it leaps over the desert floor at night. _____

6. Bactrian camels are camels with two humps. _____

7. Like the one-humped Arabian camels, Bactrian camels can go without food or water for long periods of time. _____

8. Camels get thin without water, but they quickly regain their normal weight after drinking. _____

9. Dromedaries are a breed of Arabian camels which are used for riding. _____

10. When desert donkeys find water, they can drink over 8 gallons in just a few minutes. _____

11. The male sand grouse wades in a pool until its breast feathers are full of water. _____

12. When the sand grouse returns to its nest in the desert, the chicks suck the water from its feathers. _____

13. Deserts receive less than 9.75 inches of rain each year, so the animals living there survive without much water. _____

14. A year's rainfall may come in one big storm lasting several days. _____

PART B: THE PARTS OF THE SENTENCE

EXERCISE 43: SENTENCE COMBINING

Effective writers often vary the structure of their sentences. They use a combination of **simple**, **compound**, **complex** and **compound-complex** sentences. In the space provided, combine the following sentences into one good sentence. Pay attention to **subordination**, so that the more important ideas are placed into principal clauses and the less important ideas are placed into subordinate clauses. At the end of each sentence, note the kind of sentence you have written. You may use phrases instead of subordinate clauses if you wish.

1. The kit fox has huge ears. Its ears help it to stay cool. It lives in deserts.

   _____

   _____

2. Kit foxes eat small animals. They eat rabbits. They eat lizards. They trap their food at night.

   _____

   _____

3. Oryx are antelopes. They run fast. They live in deserts. They live in Africa. They live in Arabia.

   _____

   _____

4. Ground squirrels do not live in trees. They live in burrows. These burrows are in the sand. Hundreds of ground squirrels live together. They live in colonies.

   _____

   _____

PART B: THE PARTS OF THE SENTENCE

EXERCISE 44: SENTENCE COMBINING

Combine the following short sentences into the one kind of sentence indicated. Write your answer in the blank space provided.

1. Japan consists of a chain of islands. It is a long chain. There are four main islands. There are more than 4 000 smaller islands. **Complex**

   _____

   _____

2. Most of Japan is mountainous. Over two-thirds is covered with forest. **Compound**

   _____

   _____

3. Most Japanese people live on Honshu. Honshu is a large island. Honshu has many large cities. **Complex**

   _____

   _____

4. Tokyo is the capital of Japan. 27 million people live there. Tokyo is situated on the island of Honshu. **Complex**

   _____

   _____

5. Japan produces most of its own food. This includes rice. It also includes fish. Japanese people do not eat as much meat as North Americans. **Compound**

   _____

   _____

EXERCISE 45: FORMING SENTENCES

Create a single **compound** sentence out of each sentence fragment listed below. Write your answer in the blank space provided.

1. going to the zoo and feeding the animals _____

   _____

2. Dad went to Japan, I stayed home _____

   _____

3. Mary Shelley's novel *Frankenstein*, movie of *Dracula* _____

   _____

4. recorded by the Backstreet Boys, used in an airband show _____

   _____

5. Japan's industries and manufacturing, high tech sound and video equipment _____

   _____

6. tourist attractions, excellent accommodations in Japan

   _____

   _____

7. Mount Fuji near Tokyo, Osaka Castle_____

   _____

PART B: THE PARTS OF THE SENTENCE

EXERCISE 46: FORMING SENTENCES

Create a single **complex** sentence out of each sentence fragment listed below. Write your answer in the blank space provided. Note that these are the same fragments used in exercise 48.

1. going to the zoo and feeding the animals _____

_____

2. Dad went to Japan, I stayed home _____

_____

3. Mary Shelley's novel *Frankenstein*, movie of *Dracula* _____

_____

4. recorded by the Backstreet Boys, used in an airband show

_____

_____

5. Japan's industries and manufacturing, high tech sound and video equipment _____

_____

6. tourist attractions, excellent accommodations in Japan _____

_____

7. Mount Fuji near Tokyo, Osaka Castle _____

_____

PART B: THE PARTS OF A SENTENCE

REVIEW TEST #8: KINDS OF SENTENCES *(10 marks)*

Identify the following sentences as **simple**, **compound**, **complex** or **compound-complex**. Write your answer in the blank space provided.

1. Papua New Guinea was an Australian territory until 1975. _____

2. Most people live in small villages where they grow their own food and raise animals. _____

3. Many communities have little contact with the outside world, so people have kept their own languages and traditions. _____

4. The people in Papua New Guinea speak over 700 different languages, more than any other country in the world. _____

5. Although there are several chains of islands in Papua New Guinea, the main land area consists of half the island of New Guinea. _____

6. The main island is covered in jungle, but the land is surrounded by swampy plains. _____

7. Port Moresby, the capital of Papua New Guinea, is an interesting town which tourists are now discovering. _____

8. Many people collect the stamps of Papua New Guinea. _____

9. The first stamps of Papua New Guinea were issued in 1952, but before that both Papua and New Guinea had separate stamps. _____

10. The stamps are colorful and popular because they tell us a great deal about the way of life in this remote country. _____

PART B: THE PARTS OF THE SENTENCE

ANSWERS TO EXERCISES ON KINDS OF SENTENCES

Exercise 42: *(page 90)*

1. simple
2. complex
3. simple
4. complex
5. complex
6. simple
7. simple
8. compound
9. complex
10. complex
11. complex
12. complex.
13. compound
14. simple

Exercise 43: *(page 91)*
Answers may vary.

Exercise 44: *(page 92)*
Here are some possibilities; there may be other acceptable choices:

1. Japan, which consists of a long chain of islands, has four main islands and more than 4,000 smaller ones.
2. Most of Japan is mountainous and over two-thirds is covered with forest.
3. Most Japanese people live on the large island of Honshu, which has many large cities.
4. 27 million people live in the capital of Japan, Tokyo, which is situated on the island of Honshu.
5. Japan produces most of its own food, including rice and fish, but Japanese people do not eat as much meat as North Americans.

Exercises 45, 46: *(pages 93, 94)*
The possibilities are endless. Students should ensure that each simple sentence or clause has both a subject and a verb.
Here are some possibilities: My class is going to the zoo. I read Mary Shelley's novel <u>Frankenstein</u>.

Review Test#8: *(page 95)*

1. simple
2. complex
3. compound
4. simple
5. complex
6. compound
7. complex
8. simple
9. compound
10. complex